YOU'RE ONE IN A MILLION, GRANDPA!

The C.R. Gibson Company
Norwalk, Connecticut

Dear
Grandpa
thanks
for
the
fun
I will
always
remember
this
year!
Sincerely
Shari
Enger

P.S. I Love You

You're a very important man in my life, Grandpa! Just for you, a book to celebrate everything you mean to me...

SO WILL I

My grandfather remembers long ago
the white Queen Anne's lace that grew wild.
He remembers the buttercups and goldenrod
from when he was a child.

He remembers long ago
the white snow falling falling.
He remembers the bluebird and thrush
at twilight
calling, calling.

He remembers long ago
The new moon in the summer sky
He remembers the wind in the trees
and its long, rising sigh.
And so will I
        so will I.

              CHARLOTTE ZOLOTOW

Josh Drake, Jr. recalls the magic of "down in the pasture" and the magic that was Grandpa.

Down in the pasture at Grandpa's was a straw stack, a mountainous one that drew us kids like flies. Other grownups would say we were ruining the stack, but Grandpa would just laugh, a big booming laugh, and say: "Keeping a youngster off a straw stack is almost a sin. Why, it's like keeping water away from a thirsty man."

There was Grandpa for you. He was a big, bald-headed man of Irish-Swedish-German descent, with a white cowhorn mustache. His hands were as big as hams, and his voice boomed like a 12-gauge shotgun. The whole house seemed to shake when he laughed, and the more grandkids he had around him, the louder he laughed.

I recall how we used to drive up the hill to Grandpa's big house in our Model T sedan. The yard overflowed with relatives' cars; dogs and cousins ran in every direction.

Grandma was there, small, quick, loving a houseful of kinfolk to pamper and fuss over. (She had 11 children.)

But it was Grandpa who made it a magic place.

I remember one Sunday when about 20 of us cousins chose up sides and went down into Grandpa's cotton patch, and started a cotton-boll fight. The bolls were at that hard stage before they opened, ideal for chucking, as hard as green apples and almost as big. Best of all, they'd sting when you were hit, but wouldn't break the skin. We were having a regular war, when two of my uncles ran up and ordered us out.

It seems like yesterday. Grandpa yelled from the barn. It was half a mile away, but you could have heard him twice that far, and he hollered: "Leave those kids alone!" Afterwards, I heard him say, "They could throw for an hour and not destroy over four or five dollars' worth—and they're having a thousand dollars' worth of fun."

God gave us our memories
so that we might have
roses in December.
JAMES M. BARRIE

My grandfather was like a rock
and like a tree and like an eagle.
I found, too, another likeness in him;
when I went adventuring through
these hills with him it always seemed
as if I went adventuring with God.
I think the hills were higher then.

HUGH MacNAIR KAHLER

The happiest people
are those who touch
life at the greatest
number of points.

WILLIAM MOULTON MARSTON

CHILD'S EYE VIEW

To children, intensely interested in the world around
them, everything is fresh and new. They bring this to
grandparents. I studied a caterpillar from a stomach
view with Linda . . . the brown-oranges became a
design . . . the hunching walk fascinating. Another day
we used a long-abandoned woodburning set to help
Laurie make wooden tags with wire loops to identify
by name the shrubs and trees on our place. Linda
helped hang them (low level). On outings both girls
delighted in calling out blue spruce, birch, linden tree
from their new knowledge.

During the children's visits the bird feeder overflowed
with seeds. What fun at breakfast to watch a blue jay
fall inside the container in his greed for sunflower seed,
then watch him frantically claw out. Grampa ruefully
watched seeds sprout in his fine lawn until little fingers
eagerly tugged out the weeds with him.

On evenings too chilly for late swims, Grampa took
Laurie fishing by a shady willow while Linda romped
with me on our nearest beach. Laurie loved her child-
size spinning rod Grampa taught her to use.

Because you're involved, not merely paying a visit, the inner secrets of children's thoughts spill out. Arms squeeze you hard, trusting eyes look to see what you'll do. Children need to know you inside, just as you do them. Gramma becomes someone who can be trusted and turned to, not someone who arrives with gifts and soon takes off. When Grampa thanks God at the table not only for food, but for guidance during the day, small ones become aware that God is for real, reinforcing the values taught by the parents.

Finally the visit is over. The cot goes, revealing a lost lens from Hugh's sunglasses, a squashed dolly and missing puzzle piece. But not gone are the little ones. The feel of a tiny hand on mine, a wet goodnight kiss linger. Summer will come again and with it a tiny figure stalking to the bathroom for the seventh time, a leg dangling from a tumbled bed, a refrigerator door decked with bright drawings, and whoops of "Hi Grampa" at suppertime. Another summer will come and another camp-in. Delightful!

CEIL McLEOD

JOYS OF FATHERHOOD . . .
AND GRANDFATHERHOOD

Every child is a new beginning.

What father can forget the morning when he and his son went fishing together for the first time, the boy's delight when he landed his first fish . . . the memory of his daughter's thirteenth birthday, when she wore her first long dress?

The day a child leaves for college, the day he or she graduates, the day a son or daughter marries, begins a career, and an independent but connected way of life —the joy of these tremendous milestones in a father's life cannot be indicated in words.

And finally, there is the deep pleasure of the start of a new life cycle; the phone rings one morning, and a son or son-in-law announces the arrival of a child. Once again the stress, the responsibility, and the joy begin, for the young father this time.

And for the grandfather, there is the culmination of his life's work as a father—the deep satisfaction of a hard job responsibly accomplished.

KARL MENNINGER, M.D.
SAM E. HOWIE, M.D.

THE CERTAINTY OF CHANGE

It is best to live in a land of four seasons. I have to say this firmly every March because then come days when I would gladly forfeit the beauty of New England's May and the glory of our October just to be either warm or cold, wet or dry, the year around. March can try a man's soul. But it can also make him exult, on an occasional day; and then I wouldn't willingly give up one minute of it.

If I try to pin this down, find some logic in what is obviously an emotional response and a sensory reaction, the best I can do is say that March is essentially a promise, a satisfying process in the constant state of change. This isn't really definitive, of course, since time and life are constantly changing and every season, in that sense, is a kind of promise of something different tomorrow or next week. But if I go on and say that there is more satisfaction, and even excitement, in beginnings than there is in endings, I am at least approaching an explanation.

A January snowstorm has excitement and, in one sense, satisfaction. It is a seasonal achievement. But its excitement is based on the depth of the snow, the degree of the cold, the strength of the wind, and the duration of the storm. Such a storm is primarily a challenge, but not an enduring challenge. I know from experience that the wind will ease off, the cold will moderate, the storm will end, and eventually the snow will melt. Beyond the enduring mystery of the snowflake and the aching beauty of a snowdrift, such a storm leads to nothing more than renewal of the ground water in the country and costly inconvenience in the city.

A series of hot July days also has excitement, particularly when they build atmospheric tension that explodes into thunderstorms that shake the hills and roar through the woodlands. There is satisfaction in seeing how July heat inspires the corn to reach for the sky, in the spectacular proof on every hand of the urgency of growth and ripeness. But thunderstorms pass, the green leaf proceeds with its quiet miracle of photosynthesis, the blossom is fertilized and becomes a pod or a berry or a pome or an ear. Those who live with the land tend to look upon this with the satisfaction of personal accomplishment, but we know most of these things would happen even if we sat in the shade and didn't turn a hand. What happens in July was established in March.

And right there is the reason for the countryman's response, on one of those rare but perfect March days. It is as simple as the delight in new discovery of an idea. I make the distinction, new discovery, not new idea, because what is happening in March is as old as the changing seasons themselves. It is new only as we see it again, fresh and almost innocent. There it is, the whole span of tremendous possibilities, incredible potentials, discovered afresh on a fine March day.

HAL BORLAND

grandpa in march

goes around
        the house
                each
                day

and feels the
        ground
and pinches
                twigs
and   *digs*
and   *digs*

PUSHING
spring
ARNOLD ADOFF

DEAR FOLKS: WE'RE COMING AND BRINGING THE KIDS!

How do grandparents manage when little grandchildren come to visit? It's an age-old problem, and for contemporary insight into it *Changing Times* interviewed a typical well-qualified elder, veteran of five homecomings to date.

Would you sum up your experience so far, please?
Well, I've won four and lost one, which isn't bad.

How do you figure a win or loss?
A win is any two-week visit with zero to six disputes. Anything over six goes down as a loss.

What happened on the one you lost?
That's the one where we discussed politics and toilet training.

How do you prepare for each visit?
You don't need to do much if you anticipate the critical problems. In our case, for example, we test the washing machine and dryer at least a week before; move the vacuum cleaner from the basement to the dining room; put away the ashtrays and bric-a-brac; and lay up a three-month supply of candy.

Three months? Do they usually stay that long?
Oh, no. that's for a two-week visit.

Do you do anything else?
We sleep a lot.

And when they finally arrive, you're all set to have fun with your grandchildren?
You might say fun is the hard core of the visit. My wife and I have fun in shifts. As soon as she's played out, I take over. Then she spells me, and so on. The grandchildren's parents are another matter. They're not as easy to have fun with, so you need to play it cool, as we say nowadays.

What do you mean by playing it cool?
We use a basic psychiatric approach. The idea is to listen and nod. You avoid appearing uninterested or senescent by occasional remarks such as, isn't that interesting, really, you don't say, or—best of all—I didn't know that. Incidentally, keep away from expressions such as wow, heavy and ripoff.

Wouldn't those mod words create closer rapport?
Definitely not. Young folks don't like you to trespass on their vocabulary, although I must say I never mind when they use ours.

How do you keep everyone busy during the visit?
Mostly by eating. In addition to the three regular meals, we schedule morning and afternoon coffee breaks, and a late night potluck buffet from the refrigerator.

That doesn't seem to leave time for anything else.

Well, we sit with the grandchildren a few nights so their parents can go out. That gives both couples time to complain about the other's idiosyncracies. Sort of an escape valve. And, of course, there's always shopping. The older grandchildren love to get lost in shopping centers so it's fun for everyone.

What about all the chores, such as diapers, dishes and general cleaning up?

I'm glad you brought up diapers. I've noticed that the changing job usually goes to the adult with the most highly developed sensitivities. And in these days of women's lib, men are no longer exempt. When I detect something amiss, I just tell myself that small children really don't mind those things the way we do so it can easily wait until some more fastidious adult comes along.

How do you go about recuperating after the visit?

You can't start right away, naturally. As soon as they leave, we collect the things they forgot and put them with the things they forgot on previous visits and we forgot to tell them they forgot. Then we pick the chocolate out of the upholstery. My wife got a government booklet on that, which we find very helpful.

So, after an hour or so you're ready to take a nap?

Are you kidding? Have you ever done any chocolate picking?

All of the pleasure and none of the responsibility?
Leaves from a grandfather's summer journals.

AIRY, AIRY, QUITE CONTRARY

All winter they've been simply frantic
To wallow in their own Atlantic.
They've chattered shrill of how they crave
To plunge beneath the curling wave;
With pagan fervor they exalt
The feel of sand, the tang of salt.
Comes summer and they ride with glee
Hundreds of miles to reach the sea.
What then? The ocean is too cool;
They seek the nearest motel pool.

THEIR STOMACH IS BIGGER THAN YOUR EYES

We must not irritation feel
When children gorge before the meal.
The reason why is manifest—
That's when they are the hungriest.

APPREHENSION

Whose child is this with sodden clothes
And sneezing fits and runny nose?
Its temperature is ninety-nine;
I only know if it were mine
A steaming tub I'd soak it in
And leave the rest to aspirin.
The child does not belong to me,
I'm just a scrupulous trustee,
So I must call the doctor in
Who'll grunt, and order aspirin.

OGDEN NASH

MY DEN

I have, like other lucky men,
A study, cubbyhole, or den,
A nook for work and quiet, kept
For my exclusive use, EXCEPT:
When all its closet-room and floorage
Is commandeered for trunks and storage;
Or when some inspiration-thwarters
Select the place for parking quarters;
Or when, despite my perturbation,
'Tis seized for cards or conversation,
Or occupied for sewing, knitting,
Designing hats, or garment-fitting.

With such provisos, be it known
I have a room that's all my own!

ARTHUR GUITERMAN

A knack for fun, and making a child feel special. High grandfatherly art, and Leo Rosten's father was a master at it.

When I had children, my father would tell them silly stories they were young enough to marvel over, and old enough to find the "catch" in. He would sigh, "Ah, when I was your age, I could raise my hand all the way up to here" (raising his hand above his head) "but now, I can only raise it up to here" (holding his arm out shoulder-high).

The child would frown and wrinkle his or her brow, and wonder what was—what *had* to be—wrong.

"Oh, yes," my father would say, giving the child time to penetrate the deception, "it's very sad. Imagine not being able to raise your hand higher than this—when I used to be able to raise it way up to here—"

And then a shrill voice would cry, "But Grampa, look, you just *did*!"

"Did what?"

"Raised your hand up there!!"

"Sure. That's how high I *used* to——"

"No, no, Gramps, you did it *now*!"

"Oh, I can't raise it this high now——"

"But *zayde*, look, you *are*. You're doing it!"

And he would pretend that he saw their point, or would slap his forehead to complain that he had been taken in by his own gullibility, or he would marvel how he had never before realized the absurd self-contradiction of his gesturings, or he would thank the furiously cerebrating child for such a lesson in reasoning; or he would simply laugh, and when the child looked sheepish over having been gulled, my father would deliver the swift reward of a proud hug or kiss, or a lift high in the air, or a magnified admiring or mock-rueful remark like, "My! You're too smart to be fooled."

SHIRTSLEEVE PHILOSOPHY

Leave the flurry
To the masses;
Take your time
And shine your glasses.

OLD SHAKER VERSE

I'VE GOT A NEW BOOK FROM MY GRANDFATHER HYDE

I've got a new book from my Grandfather Hyde.
It's skin on the cover and paper inside,
And reads about Arabs and horses and slaves,
And tells how the Caliph of Bagdad behaves.
I'd not take a goat and a dollar beside
For the book that I got from my Grandfather Hyde.

LEROY F. JACKSON

NIGHTTIME

Wrapped up by the night
It's cold
Where there are no lights on
I know everyone in sight
I'm warm
I've got my flipflops on
My Poppa's going to read a book
To me
It's one I know by heart
I do not need to look
To see
He's coming to the scary part
And when I go to bed
I'll dream
But I don't know which kind
Just somewhere in my head
I'll hear
The stories that are on my mind.

NINA PAYNE

Fun, according to John Bailey is teaching your grandson about fly-fishing — or grammar as the case may be. Does the following conversation sound familiar?

That evening after supper I filled my pipe and went out into the backyard. Wilbur was whipping his new rod around in the air.

"Well, Wilbur," I said, "how do you like your new fishing rod?"

"It can't be much good," said Wilbur, eyeing it suspiciously. "They admit it's split already."

"'Split-bamboo' is merely a technical term, Wilbur," I said. "This is a very good simulated split-bamboo rod, suitable for fly-fishing. You have never done any fly-fishing."

"I haven't?"

"No."

"I've done lots of fishing."

"But not with a reel."

"A real what?"

"A rod and reel. You'll find it's very different."

"Still, I'm not a new beginner."

I have to watch Wilbur's grammar all the time.

"The word 'beginner', Wilbur," I said, "should not be qualified by 'new'."

"It shouldn't?"

"No. It's redundant."

"I thought it might be."

"There is no such thing as a new beginner."

"How about one that's just started?"

"All right," I said. "Would you like me to show you some of the fine points of casting flies?"

"If it doesn't strain you to think of them," nodded Wilbur.

He handed me the rod.

"You are fortunate," I said, "to have someone present who is versed in the art."

"You are worst in the art?"

"No. 'Versed.' Fly fishing is the most artistic form of angling, Wilbur. Watch this."

I demonstrated the various details of flycasting for about fifteen minutes, then:

"Wilbur," I said, "how are the fish biting in Cooper Creek?"

"Okay, I guess."

"How would you like to go fishing there tomorrow?"

"I don't know but what I would," said Wilbur.

Again I felt I should correct Wilbur's grammar.

"'But what' should not be used for the conjunctive expression 'but that,' Wilbur," I said.

"It shouldn't?"

"No."

"Why not?"

"Because the relative cannot be disposed of grammatically."

"If you're planning to dispose of a relative," said Wilbur, "I'll go get a gunny sack."

This grandfather was a gardener . . .

Gardeners, whatever their era or locale, are of the earth earthy. They garden out of love. Such was my Grandpa Griffith. His garden was his passion and his pride. It was always as neat as a Grant Wood painting, its products blue-ribbon winners at the county fair. To him it was vital that vegetables be sown on Good Friday, and potatoes be planted dark of the moon. "When the moon comes out they sprout," he solemnly averred. Although we tended to spurn this as superstition we did so at our own risk. His potatoes *did* get to the table first, and always grew big and firm. Likewise, his radishes, green onions, and lettuce generally out-distanced all rivals. And certainly surpassed ours . . .

Potato vines (like tomatoes) have starry blossoms, and potatoes are fun to dig. Grandpa always used a pitchfork, since the blade of spade or hoe was likely to slice them in two. I can see him yet, tall and handsome and white-moustached, the clods raining softly through his lifted tines, a few potatoes clinging to the parent root like small brown gnomes. The rest were buried treasure scattered about, and you hunted them with almost the same anticipation as you hunted eggs. These first little new potatoes had skin so fragile it could be scrubbed off with a stiff brush. The flesh underneath was rosy, exactly like that of children whose mother has washed their faces too hard.

MARJORIE HOLMES

Humorist Will Stanton never forgot the stories his father and grandfather used to tell about their boyhood. What kind of memories will his sons carry with them? Not what you might expect . . .

I got to thinking the other day that boyhoods sure aren't what they used to be.

"You know," I said to Maggie, "your typical boyhood doesn't amount to a hill of beans these days. You ever think of that?"

She said yes, she thought about it a lot. All the time. I knew she was only saying it to make me feel good.

"Look at Daniel Boone," I said, "killed a bear when he was only about eight. Look at Huckleberry Finn. Look at Penrod."

"I'm looking," she said.

"Now look at me. The other morning at breakfast I was telling a story about when I was a boy. Sammy went over and began playing with the cat. Roy started reading the back of a cereal box."

"Oh well," she said, "the first thing in the morning—"

"When my father was telling a story about his boyhood we used to hang on every word. We couldn't get enough of his stories. And my grandfather. And now—"

"You shouldn't take everything so personally."

I went over to the sink and got myself half a glass of water. "I wasn't thinking of myself—it's the kids. I'd like to give them some bright childhood memories while there's still time. Something they can look back on with pride.

I called the boys into the room. They looked at me

and at each other. "We haven't done anything," Roy said.

I looked at Maggie. "You see?" I turned back to them. "Boys," I said, "what kind of childhood would you say you've had? So far?"

Roy said he thought about average.

Sammy said his childhood would be okay if he had a minibike and a lot more pizza.

"Okay," I said, "looking back, what stands out in your memory? What are some high spots?"

They took a moment to think and then they both started talking at once. A Valentine party, staying up late to watch *King Kong*, going to camp, the time I backed into the grape arbor, pulling taffy—I told them to stop. It was such a pathetic little parade of memories I couldn't stand it. I told them to go out and play.

"What can I do?" I asked Maggie. "How can I give them memories to take into their later years?"

"Take them to Altoona on a bus," she said. "That's something you don't forget."

Every season has its games. Football is a favorite of the grandfather generation.

The football season has officially begun, and in living rooms all over the nation friends are gathering to watch these exciting contests on TV.

There is a certain one-upmanship in football TV watching that has become part of the game.

If you are the host, it goes something like this.

Bradlee comes in and sits down. "What's wrong with your color?"

"It looks fine to me," you say.

"You have too much green. The players all look sick." Bradlee goes over and adjusts the color knobs. "There," he says, "that's better."

Two minutes later Dalinsky arrives. "Why is the grass so red?" he asks.

"Because Bradlee said it was too green."

"How can grass be too green?" Dalinsky asks.

Bradlee replies, "The grass is too green when the players are too green."

"I'll fix it," Dalinsky says. He gets up and twists a dial.

"It's fine now," you say, having missed the first seven plays.

Geyelin arrives and asks, "Do you still have that old TV?"

"It's not old," you protest. "I bought it two years ago."

"Where's your fine tuner?" Geyelin asks as he goes up to the set.

"It's the third button down."

Geyelin twists the fine tuner. The color comes in perfect, but he's lost the sound.

"Will you get the sound back?" Califano yells.

"If I get the sound back, everything will look yellow," Geyelin says.

"It wasn't yellow until you started fooling with it," you say. "Will you sit down so we can watch the game?"

Califano asks, "Do you have an aerial on the set?"

"Of course I've got an aerial on the set."

"Outdoors or indoors?"

"Outdoors, dammit. What kind of question is that?"

"You should be able to get Channel 7 better than that," Califano says. "Maybe there are leaves clogged in it."

"There are no leaves clogged in it," you say angrily. "I had a perfect picture before you guys came in."

"Why don't we go to my house?" Dalinsky suggests. "I have no trouble getting Channel 7."

"I don't have any trouble either," you shout.

"Then why is Howard Cosell's face chartreuse?" Geyelin asks.

"His face is always chartreuse," you reply. "That's what makes him such a good sportscaster."

Bradlee gets up and starts fiddling with the dials.

The picture goes black and white.

Everyone starts yelling at once.

Geyelin gets up and pushes another dial. The vertical is now moving sixty frames a minute.

Dalinsky gets up, stops the vertical, but now the players are elongated and look twelve feet high.

"This sure is a crazy set," Califano mutters as he tries to get the horizontal back.

"Everyone sit down," you scream. "The next person who touches the set leaves the house."

You get up and adjust the knobs exactly as they were before anyone arrived. It's a perfect picture. You sit back and suddenly you hear Frank Gifford's voice. "And that's the end of the exciting first half. Now stay tuned to a wonderful halftime show, right after this message."

ART BUCHWALD

What age would you like to be? Richard Armour asks the question and gets some surprising answers.

One of our favorite indoor sports, requiring neither physical exertion nor much intellectual activity, is to sit around and ask one another "How old (or young) would you like to be if you could pick an age?"

"Oh, to be seventy again!" exclaimed a friend of mine who is eighty-two. He is a vigorous, virile type, with a lively sense of humor.

"I'd like to be anything but a teenager," one woman said firmly. "I couldn't go through it again especially these days, with drugs and all the rest." She, I happen to know, is in her late seventies.

"I wouldn't want to be a year younger," still another said, a woman who is right around sixty-seven. "I'd hate to live my life all over. I might not do as well the next time."

None of my friends mentioned wishing to be twenty-one. This disappointed me, because I wanted to quote a piece of verse I wrote recently based on A. E. Housman's famous "When I was one-and-twenty." This is the way (not a very long way) it goes:

> *When I was one-and-twenty*
> *I knew the answers well,*
> *And anyone who listened*
> *I'd very quickly tell.*

I knew the right and wrong then,
The error of men's ways.
I never was mistaken
Back in those golden days.

I knew the world had problems;
They caused me, though, no fright.
For I, if just they asked me,
Could quickly set them right.

When I was one-and-twenty,
Impatient, restless, keen,
I was as sure, all-knowing
As those today eighteen.

As for myself, I find the answer complicated. Being the greedy type, I want the perspective and accumulated knowledge of age and the physical attributes of youth. I want the memories of the past that come with age but I also want youth's prospect of a long future in which to accomplish certain things for myself and also to see what happens to my grandchildren and the world and the human race in the next half-century or so.

CONSOLATION FOR BALDNESS

What's the advantage of hair, anyhow?
It blows in your eyes and it flops on your brow,
Disguising the shape of your scholarly head;
It often is gray and it sometimes is red.
Perhaps it is golden and ringleted, but
It needs to be combed and it has to be cut,
And even at best it is nothing to boast of
Because it's what barbarous men have the most of;
Then challenge your mirror, defiant and careless,
For lots of our handsomest people are hairless.

ARTHUR GUITERMAN

FROM GENERATION TO GENERATION . . .

Janos Koscka is a retired cabinetmaker who learned his craft as a youth in his native Hungary. Peter, his nine-year-old grandson, is learning woodburning from him on the lathe in the basement of the Koscka's two-family house on the west side of Chicago.

In San Francisco's Chinatown, ten-year-old Kim Soong stacks rice cakes, while his sister Lin, eight, wraps them in plastic for the customers in their grandfather's teashop-bakery.

Tom Mundy is spending his 60th birthday with his seven-year-old grandson Dennis. They are sitting in comfortable silence in a rowboat in the middle of a Vermont lake, waiting patiently for the fish to bite.

These three grandfathers are sharing something precious—and unfortunately rare these days—with their grandchildren, to the benefit of both generations. Passing on skills, transmitting family history, giving the young their first chance to be of real help, or just being there in undemanding companionship—these are some of the roles grandparents have played since history began. Doing so has given a fuller meaning, an extra dimension to the lives of young people and older ones, too. In fact, it is what makes a family a family.

RITA KRAMER

LIFE IS FULL OF UNFORGETTABLE FIRSTS

Your first picture with a big string of little fish or one big fish. Your first glimpse of "dogdom's aristocracy" at a dog show. The first time your lighter worked the first time for a lady's cigarette.

The first time a girl beat you at ping-pong. Your first ringside seat at a big prizefight half a block from the ring. Your first snowman admired by your first born. The first time you heard the dawn chorus of bird songs, fortissimo.

Your first ringside seat at a cabaret floorshow with the talent within pinching range. Your first ride in a car with the top down. The first time you ever tossed a nickel to an organ-grinder's monkey. Your first May basket from the opposite sex.

Your first realization that people don't go to the races just to see the horses run. Your first plunge into a railroad tunnel. (What variety the world offers if you aren't too blase!)

Your first glimpse of an oriental woman with a jewel in her nose. Your first close-up of newly hatched birds in a nest. The wedding of your first friend to marry. Your first peep at a shark in an aquarium.

Your first nervous approach to a uniformed doorman. The first time you ducked the boom (or is it spar?) on a sailboat. (You are the sum total of all the experiences you can remember.)

The first time you saw the victorious rooters tear down the goal-posts. The first time you ever suspected the artist who painted that picture might be kidding or coo-coo. The first time you ever saw a Salvation Army lass collect dimes in a bar.

Your first trayful of Christmas cards. The first time you ever caught a butterfly. Your first view of a row of colored beach parasols.

Your first sight of a mummy. Your first gazing at a faraway foreign shoreline. Your first sight in the flesh of a great baseball star. The first time you saw the beam of a 60-inch searchlight on the midnight sky.

The first time you ever moved into a new house. Your first New Year's kiss at midnight. Your first discernment of the lovely patterns of snowflakes. Your first realization that it's no disgrace to fall on your fanny at the skating pond.

Those giant flowers at your first flower show, & your first conception of breeding. Your first good report card & your dad's pride. Your first letter from a girl who had you dizzy. First encounter with a menu in French.

The first time you voted. Your first valentine to your first girl. Your first meal at an outdoor restaurant. The first time you ever got too much sunburn all at once. The first time your dad decided not to spank you.

If you jotted down all *your* big or memorable moments you could write a book.

HARLAN MILLER

ABOUT CROWS

The old crow is getting slow.
  The young crow is not.
Of what the young crow does not know
  The old crow knows a lot.

At knowing things the old crow
  Is still the young crow's master.
What does the slow old crow not know?
  How to go faster.

The young crow flies above, below,
  And rings around the slow old crow.
What does the fast young crow not know?
  Where to go.

JOHN CIARDI

HOW I SOLVE MY ENERGY CRISIS

Bob Hope shares his secrets of vim and vitality.

Everyone seems to be worrying about the energy crisis. And no wonder—it has already caused a smog shortage on the Los Angeles freeways. I wish the energy crisis had come along when I was much younger, before I had an energy crisis of my own. Actually it hasn't caught up with me yet. I'm speaking of the energy that makes *us* run—not our cars or our furnaces or our jet planes. We've all got a lifetime supply of that precious ingredient—if we just take care of it.

A lot of people have commented on my energy, and I guess for a man age 49 and holding I do have a reasonable amount of bounce to the ounce.

People often ask me how I can keep going at such a clip. (After all, I've been in show business so long I can remember when John Wayne was playing cowards.) I guess the answer is that I have been blessed with an abundance of energy, and I try to take good care of it. I don't smoke, and I drink less than Dean Martin spills. Above all, I like to stay busy. I believe that keeping active, doing what you enjoy, whether it's work or relaxation, is the secret of abundant and lasting energy.

I think another thing that has kept my energy perking is being around young people—our own four kids, the G.I. audiences I've played to for over 30 years, and the colleges I now visit. Any audience gives me a lift, but when I play for a college audience, a little of their youth and enthusiasm rubs off on me. I'm sure that anyone can profit by involving himself with young people, listening to their music, listening to *them*. We can learn a lot from the young, especially about staying young and vital.

I've found there is also a lot of restorative power in human camaraderie, in communicating, in sharing. Since I'm a ham, my idea of ecstasy is performing for 50 million people on television. But I also enjoy just talking with friends on the phone, and the way I do it, Ma Bell enjoys it, too. I like to sit around at night and call old friends all over the country. It may not be as exciting as the White House hot line, but I get a lot of warmth out of those calls.

The ability to relax is important to anyone, especially in conserving energy. And if we all laughed a little more, especially at ourselves, we'd all be more relaxed. Humor helps to relieve strain and restore energy.

In some ways, I think the present energy crisis may turn out to be a blessing in disguise. It may force many of us to leave our cars in the garage more and use our own energy to get around. Energy is self-renewing and virtually inexhaustible. It's the only thing I know that is free, legal and non-fattening—and still makes you feel great.

BREATHING PURELY

Now, at last,
I carry nothing
In my briefcase
And an empty mind.
In the meadow

Under the chestnut tree
I am a part of what I see.
Swallows above the alder thicket
Skim mosquitoes from the haze,
And I've seceded

From all committees, left
My Letters to the Editor unsent
No solutions, no opinions.
Breathing purely
Without ambitions, purged, awaiting

Annunciations of the true.
The wind is up now and the swallows gone.
I'll listen to the chestnut tree
Rustling
Empty-headed in the wind.

DANIEL HOFFMAN

Acknowledgments

The editor and the publisher have made every effort to trace the ownership of all copyrighted material and to secure permission from copyright holders of such material. In the event of any question arising as to the use of any material the publisher and editor, while expressing regret for inadvertent error, will be pleased to make the necessary corrections in future printings. Thanks are due to the following authors, publishers, publications and agents for permission to use the material indicated.

ATHENEUM PUBLISHERS, INC., for "Nighttime" by Nina Payne from *All the Day Long*. Text copyright © 1973 by Nina Payne.

CHANGING TIMES, The Kiplinger Magazine, for "Dear Folks: We're Coming and Bringing the Kids" reprinted from the February 1974 issue. Copyright © 1974 by Kiplinger Washington Editors, Inc.

THOMAS Y. CROWELL, for "So Will I" from *RIVER WINDING: Poems by Charlotte Zolotow*. Text copyright © 1970 by Charlotte Zolotow.

CURTIS BROWN, LTD., for an excerpt from *Countryman: A Summary of Belief* by Hal Borland. Copyright © 1957, 1958, 1961, 1962, 1963, 1964 and 1965 by Hal Borland.

DELACORTE PRESS, for an excerpt from *Make A Circle, Keep Us In* by Arnold Adoff. Copyright © 1975 by Arnold Adoff.

DOUBLEDAY & COMPANY, INC., for an excerpt from *The Old Familiar Booby Traps of Home* by Will Stanton. Copyright © 1962, 1963, 1966, 1975, 1976, 1977 by Will Stanton.

DANIEL HOFFMAN, for "Breathing Purely" from *Striking the Stones* by Daniel Hoffman. Copyright © 1968 by Daniel Hoffman. Published by Oxford University Press.

MARJORIE HOLMES, for "Golden Days In Grandpa's Garden" from *You and I and Yesterday* by Marjorie Holmes. Published by William Morrow & Company, Inc. Copyright © 1973 by Marjorie Holmes.

HOUGHTON MIFFLIN COMPANY, for "About Crows" from *Fast and Slow* by John Ciardi. Copyright © 1975 by John Ciardi.

ROBERT C. JACKSON, for "I've Got A New Book From My Grandfather Hyde" from *The Peter Patter Book* by Leroy F. Jackson. Copyright © 1918, 1946 by Rand McNally & Company.

LITTLE, BROWN AND COMPANY, for "Airy, Airy, Quite Contrary," "Their Stomach Is Bigger Than Your Eyes" and "Apprehension" from *There's Always Another Windmill* by Ogden Nash. Copyright © 1966 by Ogden Nash. British Commonwealth rights granted by Curtis Brown, Ltd.

McGRAW-HILL BOOK COMPANY, for an excerpt from *Going Like Sixty* by Richard Armour. Copyright © 1974 by Richard Armour.

HARLAN MILLER, JR., as executor of the Estate of Harlan Miller, for an excerpt from *There's A Man in the House* by Harlan Miller. Originally published in *Ladies' Home Journal*. Copyright © 1955 by Harlan Miller.

Photo Credits:

Selected by Barbara Shook Hazen
Designed by Thomas J. Aaron
Set in Palatino